FEATHERED DINOSAURS

BY **"DINO" DON LESSEM**
ILLUSTRATIONS BY **JOHN BINDON**

⌐ LERNER PUBLICATIONS COMPANY / MINNEAPOLIS

To Marshall Sikowitz, a great friend

Text copyright © 2005 by Dino Don, Inc.
Illustrations copyright © 2005 by John Bindon
The photographs in this book appear courtesy of: © Tom & Therisa Stack/Tom Stack & Assoc., p. 14;
© Natural History Museum of Los Angeles County, p. 15; © Dr. Philip Currie, p. 20; © The Natural History
Museum, London, p. 21.

This book is available in two editions:
Library binding by Lerner Publications Company,
    a division of Lerner Publishing Group
Soft cover by First Avenue Editions,
    an imprint of Lerner Publishing Group
241 First Avenue North
Minneapolis, MN 55401

Website address: www.lernerbooks.com

Library of Congress Cataloging-in-Publication-Data

Lessem, Don.
    Feathered dinosaurs / by Don Lessem ; illustrations by John Bindon.
        p.   cm. — (Meet the dinosaurs)
    Includes index.
    ISBN: 0-8225-1423-0 (lib. bdg. : alk. paper)
    ISBN: 0-8225-2621-2 (pbk. : alk. paper)
    1. Dinosaurs—Juvenile literature. 2. Birds, Fossil—Juvenile literature. 3. Birds—Origin—Juvenile
literature. I. Title. II. Series: Lessem, Don. Meet the dinosaurs.
QE861.5.L4765 2005
567.912—dc22   2004019651

Manufactured in the United States of America
1 2 3 4 5 6 – DP – 10 09 08 07 06 05

TABLE OF CONTENTS

MEET THE FEATHERED
DINOSAURS 4

DINOSAURS AND BIRDS 6

DISCOVERING FEATHERED
DINOSAURS 18

WHY FEATHERS? 24

GLOSSARY 32

INDEX 32

MEET THE FEATHERED DINOSAURS

WELCOME, DINOSAUR FANS!

I'm "Dino" Don. I LOVE dinosaurs. Feathered dinosaurs are some of the newest and strangest dinosaur discoveries. Come meet these amazing animals.

***ARCHAEOPTERYX* (AHR-kee-AWP-tayr-ihks)**
Length: 4 feet
Home: central Europe
Time: 145 million years ago
Most scientists think *Archaeopteryx* is a kind of ancient bird.

***BEIPIAOSAURUS* (BAY-pyow-SAWR-uhs)**
Length: 7 feet
Home: northeastern China
Time: 125 million years ago

***CAUDIPTERYX* (kaw-DIHP-tayr-ihks)**
Length: 3 feet
Home: northeastern China
Time: 125 million years ago

MICRORAPTOR (MY-kroh-RAP-tohr)
Length: 1.8 feet
Home: northeastern China
Time: 124 million years ago

SINORNITHOSAURUS (SYN-ohr-nihth-oh-SAWR-uhs)
Length: 3.5 feet
Home: northeastern China
Time: 125 million years ago

SINOSAUROPTERYX (SYN-oh-sawr-AWP-tayr-ihks)
Length: 3.5 feet
Home: northeastern China
Time: 135 million years ago

SINOVENATOR (SYN-oh-vee-NAY-tohr)
Length: 3 feet
Home: northeastern China
Time: 130 million years ago

DINOSAURS AND BIRDS

It is late in the evening, 125 million years ago. The air is cool. A little animal is spreading its tail feathers to attract another of its kind. Soft, fluffy feathers cover the animal's body and keep it warm.

What is this strange feathered animal? Is it a bird? Its name is *Caudipteryx*, and it is not a bird. It is a dinosaur—a dinosaur with feathers!

THE TIME OF FEATHERED DINOSAURS

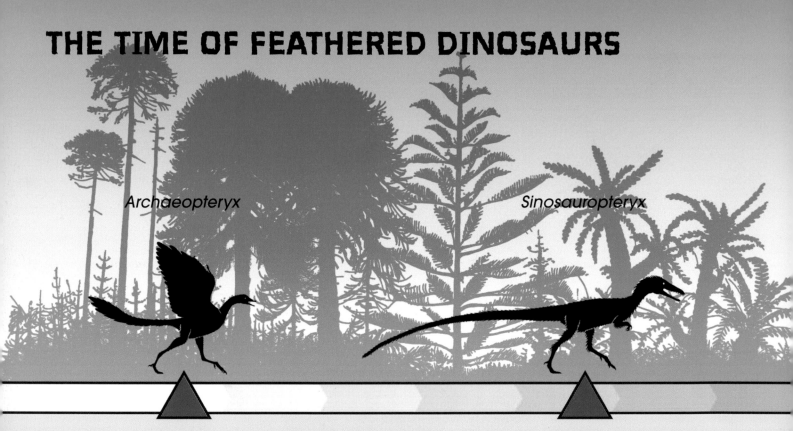

Archaeopteryx

Sinosauropteryx

145 million
years ago

135 million
years ago

Caudipteryx and other dinosaurs lived on
land millions of years ago. Dinosaurs laid
eggs, as turtles and other **reptiles** do. Some
dinosaurs had scaly skin like reptiles. But
dinosaurs were more closely related to birds.

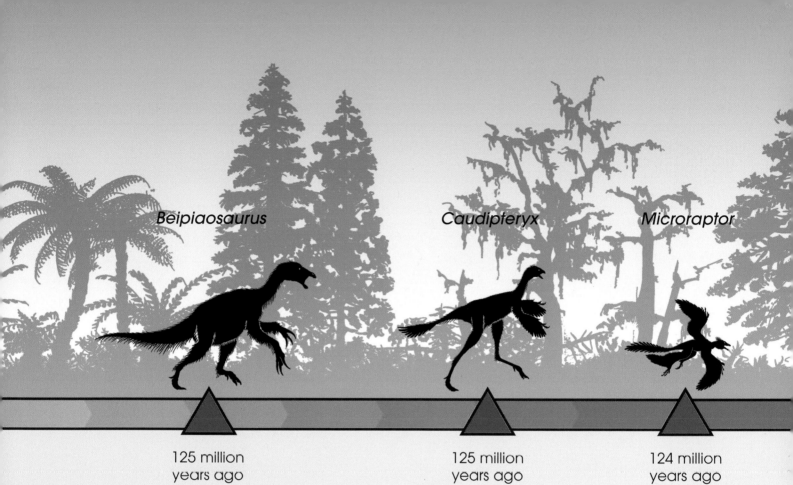

Beipiaosaurus

Caudipteryx

Microraptor

125 million
years ago

125 million
years ago

124 million
years ago

Birds and meat-eating dinosaurs were the
most alike. Both groups walked with their
legs held straight under their bodies. Both
had hollow bones. Some meat-eating
dinosaurs even had feathers.

FEATHERED FOSSIL FINDS

The numbers on the map on page 11 show some of the places where people have found fossils of the feathered dinosaurs in this book. You can match each number on the map to the name and picture of the dinosaurs on this page.

1. Archaeopteryx **2. Beipiaosaurus** **3. Caudipteryx** **4. Microraptor**

5. Sinornithosaurus **6. Sinosauropteryx** **7. Sinovenator**

We know that some dinosaurs had feathers because of **fossils.** Fossils are traces left by animals and plants that have died. Bones, teeth, and footprints left in stone help scientists understand how dinosaurs looked and lived. The best fossils show many details, such as the marks left by tiny feathers.

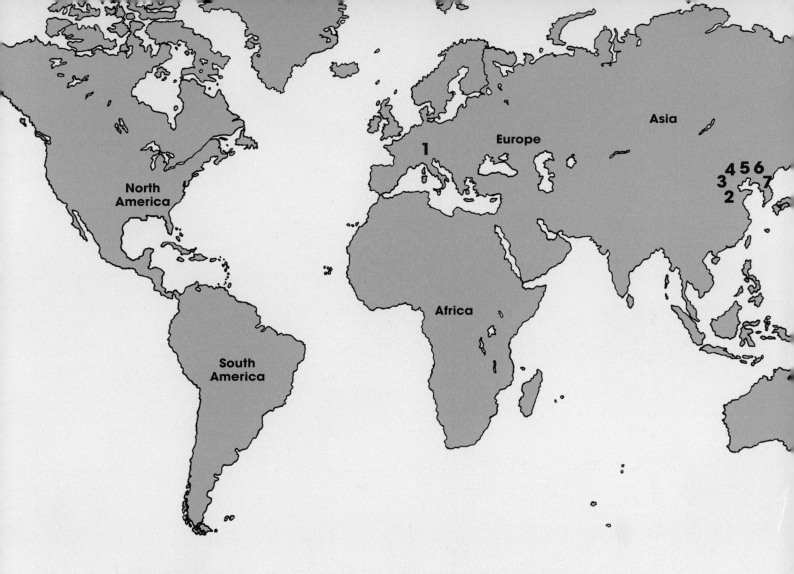

Feathered dinosaurs probably lived all over
the world. So far, scientists have found their
fossils only in China. Fossils of dinosaurs
with feathers helped change our idea of
what a dinosaur is and what a bird is.

A creature flies across a forest in Germany
145 million years ago. *Archaeopteryx*
swoops down to grab an insect for dinner.
Like meat-eating dinosaurs, *Archaeopteryx*
had hollow bones. It also had claws and
teeth like dinosaurs had.

In 1861, scientists discovered a fossil of *Archaeopteryx.* At first, they thought this animal was a dinosaur. But it had strong chest bones and feathers shaped to help it fly. Dinosaurs did not have these things. *Archaeopteryx* was the oldest bird ever found!

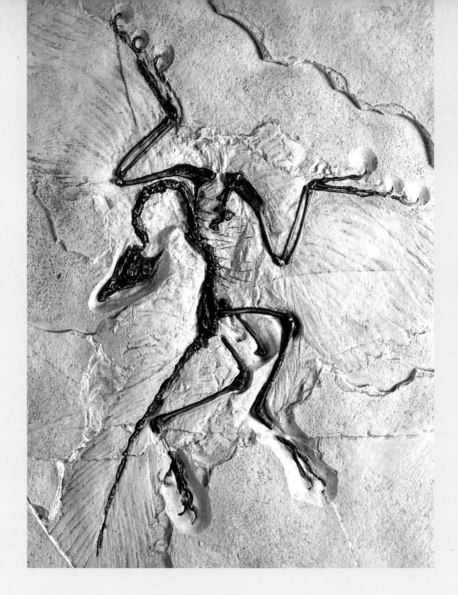

Birds from long ago, such as this
Archaeopteryx, were different from
modern birds. Modern birds have beaks
but no teeth. *Archaeopteryx* and other
birds from long ago had teeth but no beaks.

Birds in dinosaur time had wings with long
hands and clawed fingers. Most modern
birds, such as this crow, do not have claws
on their wings. Ancient birds also had
longer tails than modern birds.

Epidendrosaurus

Ancient birds and dinosaurs looked alike in many ways. Some meat-eating dinosaurs and ancient birds were about the same size. Both had long tails. And some dinosaurs had feathers.

Crow

But feathered dinosaurs are different from modern birds. The feathers of most modern birds help them fly. Dinosaur feathers did not help dinosaurs fly. The chest bones of modern birds are stronger than those of dinosaurs. Strong chest bones help birds fly.

DISCOVERING FEATHERED DINOSAURS

Millions of years ago in northern China, a volcano erupted. Many animals died. Dust gently covered the dead animals. Over millions of years, the dust turned to rock. It preserved the animals as fossils.

In 1996, scientists discovered these amazing fossils. One of the beautiful fossils they found was of a little dinosaur named *Sinosauropteryx*. It had a fuzzy covering on its body. Was this fuzz made of a kind of feather?

In 1997, scientists in Liaoning, China, made another amazing discovery. They found fossils of *Caudipteryx.* It was the most birdlike dinosaur known at that time. *Caudipteryx* had teeth that pointed forward and looked like a bird's beak.

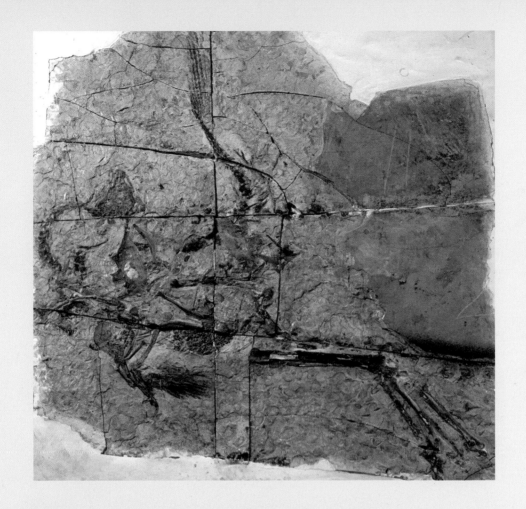

Caudipteryx also had short, powerful arms. Its arms had tiny feathers at their tips. These feathers were shaped like those of a modern bird. But the strangest part of this dinosaur was the tip of its tail. It had long feathers that might have been used to attract other *Caudipteryx.*

Another dinosaur was even more birdlike. *Sinornithosaurus* belonged to a group of small meat-eating dinosaurs with killer claws. But *Sinornithosaurus* was much smaller than *Velociraptor* and other dinosaurs in this group.

Sinornithosaurus looked a lot like
Archaeopteryx, the oldest known bird.
But this dinosaur had a thick covering
of fuzz. And *Sinornithosaurus* couldn't fly.

WHY FEATHERS?

Beipiaosaurus huddles in the cold forest. This strange feathered dinosaur was 7 feet long. It was the biggest of the birdlike dinosaurs found in China. *Beipiaosaurus* had a small head, thick legs, and a big belly. Its body was not built for flying.

Why did dinosaurs such as *Beipiaosaurus* have feathers if they couldn't fly? Perhaps feathers helped keep them warm. Plant-eating dinosaurs had big bodies to keep them warm. But the feathered dinosaurs we know of were all small meat eaters. Without feathers, the small dinosaurs might have gotten cold quickly.

Sinovenator had feathered arms and a feathery tail. But its feathers and body were not made for flying. *Sinovenator* was a small relative of *Troodon*, the smartest of all dinosaurs.

Like *Troodon, Sinovenator* had a big brain and sharp claws. It was also a fast runner. It could hunt and defend itself easily. It didn't need to fly to catch its food or to escape danger. Perhaps this dinosaur waved its arms and tail feathers to attract other adult *Sinovenator*.

Scientists used to think that no dinosaurs could fly. But new discoveries show that some dinosaurs might have flown. One of these dinosaurs was named *Microraptor*. It was no bigger than a crow.

Microraptor had long arms and legs.
Its arms and legs had feathers, so they
looked like wings. *Microraptor* might
have jumped down from trees and glided
through the air. Maybe it glided to catch
insects and lizards to eat.

About 65 million years ago, dinosaurs died out. What killed them? Scientists think that **asteroids** might have. The asteroids could have caused fires or made volcanoes erupt. Clouds of dust would have filled the air and blocked sunlight. Dinosaurs and many other kinds of animals died out at this time.

But birds did not die out. No one knows why
these relatives of the feathered dinosaurs
survived. New discoveries in China may
help us to solve this mystery. Perhaps one
day we will understand why we see birds in
our skies but no dinosaurs on our land.

GLOSSARY

asteroids (AS-tur-oydz): large, rocky lumps that move through space

fossils (FAH-suhlz): the remains, tracks, or traces of something that lived long ago

reptiles (REHP-tylz): a group of animals that have scaly skin and lungs for breathing air

INDEX

birds, 8–9, 11, 13, 14–17, 20, 21, 31

bones, 9, 10, 12, 13, 17

claws, 12, 15, 22, 27

flying, 13, 17, 23, 24–29

fossils, 10–11, 13, 18–19, 20

hunting, 12, 27, 29

reptiles, 8

size, 4–5, 16, 22, 24–25, 28

tails, 6, 15, 16, 21, 26–27

teeth, 10, 12, 14, 20

wings, 15, 29